# RE-ELECT NO ONE

# RE-ELECT NO ONE

Then New Brooms Can
Put Money On Main Street Not Wall Street

Carlton Laird

| Library of Congress Control Number: | | 2010907063 |
|---|---|---|
| ISBN: | Hardcover | 978-1-4535-0369-0 |
| | Softcover | 978-1-4535-0368-3 |
| | Ebook | 978-1-4535-0370-6 |

This book was printed in the United States of America.

**To order additional copies of this book, contact:**
Xlibris Corporation
1-888-795-4274
www.Xlibris.com
Orders@Xlibris.com
81075

# Contents

How can I make this subject interesting? Telling you our Nation is kaput, ruined, broken? This is not new to you. Most people recognized this long before a collapsed economy finally got the attention of our elected officials. Yes we need change before rigor mortis signals the death of our Founder's efforts to establish the World's first real Democracy. The Public also knows our so-called Recession will not be corrected by pouring huge amounts of the Public's money into Wall Street. In the absence of any plan of action with a reasonable chance of solving our Nation's fiscal problems this book offers an analysis of the problem and also suggests ways to correct our financial problems.

You and I know a quick fix is unlikely so let's begin to identify the problem so it can be corrected. For starters go back a couple years to candidate for President Obama's selection of Springfield, Illinois where President Lincoln once had a law office. Quite likely this site was picked to infer or induce some similarity to a great President. Now let's move forward to the last days of the George Bush administration and passage of TARP, the $700 billion "Troubled Stabilization Assets Relief Program". This should help us tie some loose strings together.

# LINCOLN SERVED THE PUBLIC—OBAMA FAILS TO DO LIKEWISE

In 1861 President Lincoln refused to commit the Nation to 25% interest the banks wanted to finance the Civil War. Fortunately Lincoln knew the Constitution and directed the Treasury Secretary to issue interest-free bonds in the amount of $450 million to finance that War. Lincoln was the first President to use Article 1 Section 8 of the Constitution the Founders had inserted to protect the new Nation from being exploited by banks. Lincoln's knowledge and action saved taxpayers millions of dollars and the Supreme Court upheld his action when it was challenged.

So how much did Lincoln save the taxpayers? Well no government has any money until it levies taxes and occasionally fees are charged for a particular service. To pay the cost of the Civil War the 1862 Congress levied an income tax of 25 cents on each $100 over $500 in income. And this tax was self-assessed with no penalties for failure to submit a return! In 1863 a salary tax was added and taxes were levied on liquor and distilleries. By 1865 the gross tax collected amounted to $308,582. (Internet) Compare this to the bank request of 25% on the $450 million the U. S. Treasurer issued in interest-free bonds. At the end of four years of War the interest banks would have collected would an amount equal to the principal of $450 million.

The application of a temporary income tax was used to finance the occasional short wars our Nation conducted in its early history. Then for WWI and WWII there were War Bond drives but the bond drive for WWII did not come close to meeting the funding needs and Public debt increased. Another procedures began with the George Bush administration and continued by President Obama; the cost of War was "off budget" and of course the Public debt escalated, to the joy undoubtedly of the Federal Reserve that collects interest on Government debt! In review the initial Government's policy was "you can have what you are asking for if you are willing to pay for it." Yes that really changed; for several decades it appeared Congress was running a tab for expenditures. Our creditors didn't complain and neither did the Public, until—2008 when our financial system collapsed. Though millions have lots jobs Wall Street is doing well on the Trillion or more tax dollars advanced to them by our Government—the Public's money! Something is very, very wrong!

President Obama could have followed Lincoln's action but chose to help bankers instead, even using the Banker-derived mantra, "Some banks are too large to allow to fail." Of course that is a myth—Obama could have acted in the interest of the people as Lincoln did by instructing the U. S. Treasurer to issue tax-free loans to any unit of government with a tax base. This would have started "shovel-ready projects" President Obama and Congress liked to mention in the early stage of the 2008-2009 Recession. Dollars given to local governments would create local jobs and put dollars on Main Street including local banks. The Wall Street financial juggernaut should have been allowed to fail but instead George Bush and Barack Obama chose to pour unbelievable amounts of the Public's money into the top and expect the "trickle down" theory to correct the Recession. It's a good guess that both Presidents Bush and Obama either failed to take Economics 101 or failed if they did. Obama didn't introduce CHANGE but repeated the old trick of pouring the Public's money in at the top to solve Recessions that does not work for it simultaneously increases Public debt.

In a perverted way Presidents Bush and Obama did follow Lincoln's method of financing the Civil War. They issued interest-free money but gave the Public's money to their friends, the banking syndicate that does not create wealth but thrives on the debts of others. If we really believe in a free enterprise financial system the Wall Street banks and their related followers, the creators of questionable schemes that create inflation, should have been allowed to fail. Main Street would not have suffered if the Public's own money had been introduced on Main Street that is a proper exercise for a Democracy. A small tax levy might have been needed at the start but as I will explain later the no-interest loans would soon result in the equivalent of recycling the Public's money.

Time and again Presidents and Congress give money, sizeable amounts to special interests and to other nations. This raises real questions within the Public and this quandary will continue until Voter Initiative and the Referendum are made available to the Public. Later in this book I point out the deficiencies in the Representative Republic-type Government established by our Pioneer settlers. That system was practical then, but today we have instantaneous communications along with a very satisfactory transportation system. We can and should be improving our governing system through public participation and that procedure will be explained later.

# AN EXCEPTION WORTH NOTING

On June 4, 1963 President John F. Kennedy issued Executive Order 11110, in effect repeating President Lincoln's action to authorize the U. S. Treasury to use its Constitutional power to issue interest-free currency. President Kennedy gave the Treasury Department authority to issue silver certificates backed by silver bullion or silver dollars in the Treasury. This currency was free of interest and debt, meaning the Federal Reserve would collect no interest on the creation and existence of this currency. By September 1963 more than 4 billion dollars in new United States Notes (currency) in denominations of two dollar and five dollars bills were put into circulation. Ten dollar and 20 dollar denomination bills were being printed when President Kennedy was assassinated November 23, 1963 and those bills were never circulated. And within a few months all of the Silver backed debt-free currency President Kennedy had authorized and was in circulation was also withdrawn. President Kennedy's new interest free notes were in competition with Federal Reserve notes Congress authorized in 1913. And the currency President Kennedy authorized was backed by real value, silver, whereas the Federal Reserve notes still in circulation are not backed by anything of intrinsic value and the Public continues to pay interest to banks for the use of the Public's own money, that of course is part of the Public Domain!

There is some belief that a conspiracy exists since Presidents, Lincoln and Kennedy the only ones to implement Article 1 Section 8 were assassinated. But whether a conspiracy did or does exist is immaterial; the Public not only has sufficient authority but also the Responsibility to insure our laws and the Constitution are upheld. However time and again abuses in government have occurred and the Public fails to act, to use the powers available. Why? I alluded to this above—it is because we maintain the antique system of a Representative Republic the Pioneers adopted only because transportation and communications did not exist in1787. Today there is no excuse for continuing a device or system that was a necessity only for a short period of history. The hazard in continuing this antique system the Pioneers adopted as a convenience soon provided an open door for special interest that have dominated our Government for decades. Small wonder there are 5 or 6 times more lobbyists in Washington than there are elected Officials!

# GOVERNED BY SPECIAL INTERESTS

So why do we cling to antique political and financial policies established more than 200 years ago when most people know these policies are sending our Country in the wrong direction? There is a standard answer to that question and most questions pertaining to Government: It is, "We have always done it that way!" A Representative Republic was practical in 1787 but the believers in a real Democracy need to be implementing Public participation in Government. Instead we put the affairs of Government on "automatic pilot" while we busied ourselves with pleasures and making money! Just voting every 2-4 years does not make a democracy, but it does make us comparable with Russia and Zimbabwe!

Granted a few minor changes have been made in Government, but not enough to prevented Congress from evolving into our own Royalty Class. And we have allowed the dominant animal drives of power and greed to support the Keystone underpinning for Wall Street. Changes that could give the Public more participation in their government have not happen but needs to happen to get the benefits of a real Democracy. This will be explained in more detail later.

Hence the title of this book seemed appropriated. The voters owe nothing to incumbents to Public office. Only in government could such demonstrated incompetence be tolerated. We the voters, and about another one-half of our population that do not vote, have allowed ourselves to be represented by a group that gives itself automatic salary increases, a Cadillac sick leave policy, retirement at full salary, and travels through out the world at taxpayer expense. We are not even offended when this group is bribed to vote for a lesser-type health plan for the public. Whether you favored or opposed the proposed the Public Health Plan is not the immediate question, but what is really upsetting is our elected officials callously ignored the Public while enjoying their own self-created Royalty status. All legislative bodies, State and federal, have completely reversed the traditional Master/Servant relationship! We the taxpayers are the Servants!

The Public owes Congress nothing and electing one, two or even a dozen new candidates will not change anything in Washington D.C. A housecleaning is necessary and the Public can begin this procedure by eliminating at least one-third of Congress by refusing to vote for all incumbents in the November 2010 election. And if this number of changes in the current number of elected officials is not enough to make the necessary changes in our Government another one-third of Congress can be removed in the 2012 election. After the

November 2010 housecleaning the replacement candidates need to understand the Public's desire is to reduce the cost and the size of the federal Government. If the Newly elected officials fail the Public's trust a recall vote needs to be considered. A vast number of residents are suffering financially from lost jobs and milquetoast measures by newly elected officials should not be tolerated.

Unfortunately a quick fix will not occur and later in this book there are suggested steps to re-establish the Democracy the Founder planned for this Country to become a unique experiment and example to the World on how freedom and Public control can be achieved. Their dream was sidelined and the cause for this failure is addressed later in this book. At this point our task ahead will be almost like starting anew but this time we will know how to avoid many previous pitfalls.

The comprehensive approach presented in this book for correcting our governing failures is addressed in three steps.

(1) Correcting the financial system, a crucial item at this time.
(2) Changes to reduce the size and cost of our federal government.
(3) Offer a plan to achieve (1) and (2).

# (1)

## Correcting Our Financial System

The Founders intended the world's first real democracy would apply democratic principles across the board—both the political and financial systems were to follow Democratic principles. This immense task began in 1787 with the drafting of our Constitution in Philadelphia. At that time freedom, as set forth by the Founders did not exist anywhere in the world! This unusual gathering of Pioneers provided the seed of a revolution in governing as our Pioneers began with a blank sheet of paper and produced the World's first Constitution! Clearly it was the resolve of an outstanding group of settlers determined to achieve freedom that made victory over the great power of England possible. Though freedom had never existed it was starting to be written about by a few philosophers and writers. Our Founders knew these writings and this probably increased their desire to be free of England's yoke of oppression. Some of those early writers on Freedom are listed below.

Roger Williams, 1603-1683, founder of the Rhode Island Colony and the first Baptist Church in the United States. Williams advocated the separation of church and state.

John Locke, 1632-1704, a philosopher that urged logic to determine Freedom. His teaching influenced Voltaire and much later in 1934 the State of Nebraska changed a bicameral of 133 legislators to the unicameral with 49 legislators reducing the annual cost of their legislature by more 50%.

Rousseau, Jean-Jacques, a Swiss philosopher, writer, and composer of the "Enlightenment" that influenced the French revolution. His works are credited with influencing Hegel and Freud. He also contributed to music as a theorist and a composer.

Thomas Hobbes, 1588-1679, a natural law philosopher who had met Galileo and was influenced by Galileo's theory on motion and planets. Galileo was later excommunicated by the Catholic Church, becoming an early victim of Change!

David Hume, 1711-1776. Philosopher and economist believed a nationís wealth was determined by its stock of manufactured goods rather than its stock of money.

Voltaire, 1694-1778, a defender of civil liberties, freedom of religion, and the right to trial by jury.

Adam Smith, 1723-1790, author of "The Wealth Of Nations" published in 1776.

—

> Appointed to the chair of moral logic, Glasgow University, lectured on free market economy for economic.

Our Founders also knew well how poverty was imposed on the public by special interests that controlled Old World finances. And this knowledge prompted the Founders to insert an antidote in the Constitution, the world's first document of its kind, for the purpose of preventing special interests dominating the finances of this new nation. That antidote is Article 1 Section 8 and states, "Congress shall have the power to coin Money and regulate the value there of."

No one can or should interpret this portion of the Constitution as permitting a privately owned banking syndicate that operates secretly, pays no taxes, and that cannot be audited as complying with Article 1 Section 8 of our Constitution. I have just described the Federal Reserve that was given control over the Public's funds along with the right to collect a fee (known as interest) on every dollar of debt created by Congress. That power given the Federal Reserve violates the Constitution. Even a Junior High Student would recognize this violation though members of Congress pledge to support the Constitution and yet few have ever objected or raised a question regarding the action of the Federal Reserve. The Federal Reserve exercises a monopoly over Public funds and are aided by collusion with a spendthrift Congress.

When the Federal Reserve was created in 1913 the Public debt was about one billion dollars. Today the National debt is a nebulous figure estimated to be around 60-70 Trillion dollars on which the Federal Reserve collects interest annually. Surprised? We shouldn't be for the Federal Reserve lives off of Public debt!

# A Light at the End of the Tunnel is Possible

If voters remove all incumbents in the November 2010 election the new Congress might have enough votes to cease paying interest on bonds that have been issued illegally by the U. S. Treasury and monetized by the Federal Reserve. The annual savings possible for taxpayers by refusing to pay interest on illegally issued bonds would amount to about a half Trillion dollars, an item occurring in each of our Nation's annual budgets. After eliminating all incumbents in the November 2010 election the test will be whether the residual remaining Royalty in Congress will join with the newly elected members of Congress to rescind the Federal Reserve Act of 1913. If this cannot be achieved our Country will have to wait until more Royalty can be removed in the 2012 election.

The metamorphism in President Obama from Candidate Obama to President Obama surprised great numbers of people as his main Cabinet selection consists of the top echelon people from Wall Street and the Federal Reserve, people that have little or no knowledge of the thoughts and wishes of the vast majority of U. S. residents. The real wealth of our Nation is produced in factories, farms, mines and other endeavors that create usable consumer items. For decades the people that now surround and advise President Obama bragged that the days of sweat jobs in our Nation are gone, replaced by people that plan and administer systems! Let the developing countries do the sweating while skyscrapers of "paper pushers" plan, or is it scheme and design new and proliferating instruments of credit. President Obama's main advisers represent banking and as stated banks do not create wealth, they exist on credit and have continually inflated credit through ephemeral schemes and illusion. Banks and government are both parasitic and neither is qualified to set policies for others.

# HOW OUR FOUNDERS NEW
# GOVERNMENT WAS DERAILED

It was noted near the beginning of this book that the absence of communications in the early days of this Nation resulted in the Founder's adoption of a Representative Republic but that system was usurped by special interests decades ago. The critical and disruptive incident that diverted the Founders intended Democracy resulted from a bank charter issued to Alexander Hamilton in 1782 by the Commonwealth of Massachusetts. That bank charter gave Old Europe's financing methods a foothold before our new nation had even started! Actually another year passed before even our War for Freedom was won in 1783 and the Constitution was not drafted and approved until 1787. That bank charter was not only untimely, it prevented democracy from ever being applied to our Nation's financial system as the Founders had intended. And as we know so well, control of our financial system by special interests is responsible for our current financial collapse and was also the cause of numerous booms and busts from the beginning of our Nation.

How could this disruptive event happen? Keep in mind the Pioneers were widely scattered throughout the New England colonies. There was no communication system and transportation was mostly by horseback with a very limited use of the stagecoach. Hamilton should be credited for being a sharp entrepreneur; he recognized the new Nation had huge debts and would need to borrow millions of dollars. He also recognized debts secured by a government are ideal because government has the power to tax all the people! That remains a critical point in our Government even today and will be discussed as we move along in this book. It was the difficulty in communication among widely scattered Pioneers that made it necessary to establish the new Government as a Representative Republic. But why haven't we recognized the era of difficult or limited communications was corrected long ago?

Instead elected officials and the Public have not questioned a 200-year-old system to fill the expectations of a modern democracy. For several decades we have had electronic communication systems that could provide the Public with the potential for Direct Democracy through Voter Initiative and the Referendum. Public needs the capability to compete with legislatures in making laws to end political deadlocks and legislation like "earmarks" that are acts of stealing and if done in any business other than government would result in a prison sentence! Participatory government is really a requirement if the Public expects Government to change. This does not mean every person needs to keep in daily touch on legislative events since in every community there are people with the interest and the time to follow governing events. What is lacking is a system that provides interested citizen the procedure for alerting others, even to initiating petitions. Step (2) of our outline will expand on this.

# FINANCIAL CONTROL—
# THE REAL SOURCE OF POWER

---

Why did our Founders insert Article 1 Section 8 in the Constitution? Not only was our Constitution new to the World but advocating democracy be applied to finances—well that remains a new concept even today for it has never been tried! The Founders had personal experience with serfdom that plagued Old Europe for centuries and they recognized the root cause of this poverty came from the philosophy of a prominent European, Mayer Amschel Rothschild who stated in 1790, "Let me control a nation's money and I care not who makes the laws". (The Internet; also repeated by a later Rothschild in 1838).

Currently no Rothschild, at least in name, controls our banking system but an alliance or association of banks deceptively named the Federal Reserve continues and has even extended the Rothschild's dictum. During the 18th and 19th century the Rothschild philosophy held forth even though kings and legislatures changed the Rothschild's dynasty maintained financial control. That dictum or theorem continues today in Washington D. C. with only a minor change made to accommodate the introduction of democracy. That "accommodation" is why we have only a pseudo or imitation democracy. All the Rothschild dictum needed to change to gain control of a democracy was to "expand" the distribution of campaign funds to elected officials! Small "change" when banking income is derived from nearly a hundred Trillion of Public debt that our elected officials helped to create! The original Rothschild dynasty would be proud that a new generation of their "believers" is now able to transfer all banking debts over to the Public, via the Federal Reserve System!

Banking income is greatly enhanced from contrived and uncontrolled debt instruments, including counterfeiting that is made acceptable with the name of "fractional reserve" legalized by Congress but was not extended to credit unions. Apparently some sacred cows are ok even in a democracy. In 1971 President Nixon gave banks a major assist by removing virtually all-banking regulations. This opened the floodgates and debt creation really took off into the "wild blue yonder". The first victim of this "run away splurge" of credit was the Savings And Loan Debacle in mid-1980s. Out of that evolved the mantra "Some banks are too big to allow to fail." Could that have been foresight or clairvoyance of bankers remembering the Boy Scout slogan "Be Prepared"? And now after Wall Street banks and their associates have driven credit beyond its breaking point our elected officials have decided the solution for our financial system is to give more power to the Federal Reserve!

Our financial system has never been controlled by the Public or publicly elected officials as required by our Constitution As a result the Public is continually "fleeced" by the collusion of elected officials and the Federal Reserve that assumed the power to transfer banking losses from mismanagement, even corruption onto the Public debt. And instead of a Nation claiming to be a democracy our Government resembles a "logrolling agreement" between Congress and the Federal Reserve.

Our Freedom as well as our system of democracy is endangered when the subject of government is deemed so unimportant it is no longer part of the curriculum in our education system. For instance few people in the U. S. understand the use and value of Voter Initiative that is the effective way to get meaningful Public participation in Government. Unless there is occasionally some degree of public participation in Government we will remain a democracy in name only, but on par with Russia and Zimbabwe that also vote every two to four years. A resident of those two nations has no control of its government but that is virtually the condition in the U. S.

A major reason the Swiss have maintained a successful Democracy for more than a century is due to their frequent use of Voter Initiative and the Referendum. California residents effectively used these methods of participating in government in the past however their current excessive State debt is due in a great part to their failure to apply citizen participation to break up a deadlocked legislature. Voter Initiative is explained in more detail in previous books "Direct Democracy" and "Oh The World Owes Us A Living".

# BENJAMIN FRANKLIN'S
# ACCURATE PROJECTION

A quotation from Ben Franklin listed below may embarrass us; his message seems even clairvoyant. Franklin understood human nature and his long and varied experience helped him to recognize a Representative Republic as a makeshift to fit only a situation of scattered Pioneers. When the Constitution was being drafted in 1787 Franklin was old and ill; he prepared a letter that was read at the Convention by a friend. Franklin wrote:

> "There is no form of government but what may be a blessing to the people if well administered, and I believe farther that this is likely to be well administered for a course of years, and can only end in Despotism, as other forms have done before it, when the people shall become so corrupted as

to need Despotic Government, being incapable of any other."

(From "We Are The Patriots" by Gore Vidal)

Some would like to think Franklin's prediction has not happened to our Nation but his analysis is too accurate to ignore.

# Preparing Our Government for the 21<sup>st</sup> Century

When the time arrives that our federal Government adopts the policy of loaning interest-free money to any governing entity with a tax base the Nation will begin the form of Government envisioned by our Founders. The next paragraph explains how issuing interest-free loans to local units of Government would work.

Residents of any governing entity would be eligible to receive an interest-free loan from the U. S. Treasury. The recipient of these funds would meet jointly with their elected officials to determine the amount of interest-free money to be borrowed and also to determine the repayment schedule for these borrowed funds. Setting a repayment schedule will be based on how much residents are willing or able to afford. It is appropriate that tax-supported communities and Districts would be funded with interest-free loans as any money held by the federal Government came from the Public, from these many local taxing units. As stated previously no Government has any money until it takes money from individuals through taxes and fees. Since all Government held money belongs to the Public it makes sense for the money to be used again and again through this procedure of recycling. Because the money is basically being recycled, from the U. S. Treasury to State and local governments and then back again to the U. S. Treasury massive federal debts will not accumulate. One other protection that is needed is the approval of Voter Initiative and the Referendum at the federal level to provide citizen participation at the national level. There will be more about this in the next section of this book.

Yes, this is a very new financial concept after decades of our Government issuing bonds that require paying interest that amounts to the Public being charged for the use of its own money. The interest paid on bonds exceeds the amount borrowed by as much as three times for 20-year bonds. And it is not uncommon for new bond issues to include unpaid portions of previous bond issues. Of course that is one reason why both federal and many State Governments are now deeply in debt.

A few decades ago the "ME generation" became a widespread belief and declared everyone has "Rights" to many things. The Constitution does provide rights "before the law" but says nothing about rights to a portion of the property and assets of others. The excess spending due to the expansion of "rights" came when elected officials decided to accommodate all demanding groups for this insured re-election. The outcome is apparent—when the well runs dry an awakening occurs. Belief in "Responsibility" is gradually returning, meaning individuals and their governments will experience less affluent lifestyles. Part of the corrections needed is for all governing units, particularly State and federal Governments, to adopt Standard accounting practices to make it possible for everyone to know their Governments financial situation at any time.

# IT IS ILLEGAL TO DEBASE OUR CURRENCY

An item of financial history explains how far "we the people" have allowed our Government to violate the sound financial principles established when our New Democracy began. The Colonies began their new federal Government with no system of money—foreign coins were the medium of exchange and were obtained by selling commodities produced to other nations. The first U. S. Mint of our new Government was not established until 1792, four years after the new federal Government began in 1788. Of interest is Section 19 of the U. S. Coinage Act of 1792 that states: " .... anyone guilty of debasing gold or silver coins or making coins worse in weight or value shall be put to death." Our paper money, our currency, was introduced later for convenience in transactions. Public confidence or sufficient faith in the ability of the issuing government to support and honor the paper currency was essential. Now consider how members of Congress and the Federal Reserve have debased the value of our money, the dollar. For decades it has been common practice for the Federal Reserve to "open the spigot" as it was called to increase the amount of currency in circulation. Of course this spurred inflation time and again resulting in bubbles that then burst, costing many people their savings. The dollar has continually decreased in value from the time the Federal Reserve was created in 1913 until today the 1913-dollar is worth less the five cents. Certainly our currency has been "debased", and is in violation of Section 19 of our Coinage Act! It is time for a thorough housecleaning in Congress!

# CLINGING TO THE PAST

Elected officials are not known for their innovation and so current stimulus policies repeat those used during the 1930's Depression. President Roosevelt generously used taxpayer funds to finance government work projects and also to bail out privately owned banks and private businesses even though there is an absence of proof Government aid solved the 1930s Depression. It was WWII that put everyone to work, solving the 1930 Depression but of course greatly increase government debt. History does not repeat exactly so another War in 2010 is not an alternative for repeating the 1930s. Candidate Obama's campaign rhetoric for change turned to disappointment when he adopted "FDR's pump priming of the 1930,s using Public funds to bail out the mammoths of Wall Street and members of the Federal Reserve to be his top advisors. There is a fitting expression for these actions: "If you keep doing the same thing over and over and expect different results to occur, it may be a sign of insanity!"

# It's the 21ST Century— it's Time for New Ideas!

And speaking of repetitive acts the Federal Reserve periodically has a technique to vacuum the savings and wealth of the entire Nation. When bank operations suffer from bad loans or other risky operations the Federal Reserve lowers interest rates to zero or near zero. Thrifty individuals that have accumulated savings are then faced with a return on their savings that is below the cost of living. These "arranged periods of zero interest" assist mismanaged banks to recoup their capital by borrowing from the Federal Reserve at zero or near zero interest and then investing the borrowed funds into Government bonds yielding from 2 to 4 percent interest. Of course the Government bonds these banks are buying in this convoluted scheme can result in increasing the Public debt, a "double whammy" for taxpayers. The ghosts of Rothschild must be smiling!

To sell the Federal Reserve Act to the 1913 Congress banks claimed the Federal Reserve system would do following:

1. Provide full employment.
2. Stabilize prices.
3. Balance international trade and payments.

Was the Act oversold? Your elected officials bought it!

It all reduces down to the fact we have never had a real, fully operating Democracy. The Swiss are much closer to a real democracy because they provide Voter Initiative and the Referendum even at the national level. Here in the U. S. we have not wanted to be bothered with government beyond voting every 2 to 4 years. In the early 20th century H. L. Mencken, a journalist and publisher described elections as, "An auction of stolen goods." Some citizen participation in government is absolutely necessary to achieve real democracy. And this would not require everyone to continually follow every event occurring in government. As noted there are people in every community with the interest and the time to keep an eye on government. These modern "Minute Men" need help from the Public to provide the mechanism like Voter Initiative and the Referendum to alert the Public when action is needed.

# (2)

## Extracting Ourselves from Our Mess

Candidates for Public offices usually promise to reduce the debt and the size of government. It never happens and for good reason. Electing one, two, even a dozen newcomers to Congress or to State legislatures cannot correct the entrenched problems in our Government. Newcomers with good intentions are either sidelined or they soon recognize the futility and decide to conform and be part of Royalty. However the Public is not helpless on this matter but a procedure needs to be put forward to help those "Minute Men take action.

RE-ELECT NO ONE in the upcoming election of November 2010 will be a good start. This could reduce the "status quo" in Congress by eliminating one-third of the established Royalty and if it turns out this amount of "housecleaning" is not enough the Public should be prepared to eliminate another one-third of the status quo in Congress in the 2012 election. We have a real mess on our hands and it will take time and persistence to correct the entrenched misdeeds that became anchored very early as the intent of the World's first real Democracy was diverted. Of course correcting our malfunctioning system will require the persistence and dedication similar to the task that our Pioneers faced in 1787. A plan is needed to serve as the nucleus for the "new brooms" after winning the November 2010 election.

As a mental exercise let's review some improvements that could reduce the cost and size of the federal Government. Currently it is common for Congress as well as State legislatures to be deadlocked for political reasons. The needs of the Public are ignored due to politics.

One alternative dates back to the 1930 Depression when U. S. Senator George Norris of Nebraska recognized the importance of reducing the cost of government and that still remains a high priority today. Senator Norris traveled his State of Nebraska and explained to voters it did not make sense for the public to elect two different legislative bodies to represent them when the dual bodies only create unnecessary delays and expense to taxpayers, as the two elected bodies eventually have to reconcile their differences in still another committee. Nebraska voters became convince and voted to adopt a unicameral government that has just one legislative body called the Senate.

In 1934 Nebraska voters changed from a bicameral legislature with 133 members to a unicameral legislature with 49 legislators. The cost reduction exceeded 50%. Local candidates for Nebraskaís unicameral legislature may file for election by Party affiliation or as Independents but if elected they serve as a non-partisan. For over 70 years a unicameral legislature has served that State and not once has there been any effort to revert back to a bicameral legislature.

So why do other 49 States and the U. S. Congress continue with bicameral legislatures? Well, "custom and tradition" and a lackadaisical Public that accepts "We Have Always Done It That Way". Whenever the Public, or at least some individual wants to reduce the cost of Government badly enough change and improvement could happen. But until then you can be very sure no politician is going to legislate itself out of a job! Unfortunately real Statesmen like George Norris do no come along every day.

While we are looking for large expenditures to reduce or eliminate let's look at State Legislatures. Why are State Legislatures always concentrated in State Capitol cities? Yes, one answer is: "Because We Have Always Done It That Way!" The real reason begins with the start of our Government in 1778. We noted before those Pioneers had no communications and transportation systems, so assembling elected officials in State Capitol cities was logical. Today communication can be instantaneous and transportation would benefit if the location of elected officials were decentralized by removing the legislature from the Capitol cities with each elected officials locating its office within the legislatorís district. Public participation would be enhanced and the ability of special interests to influence legislation would be greatly reduced. Our electronic communications, including visual pictures are available today and State and local governments would become more accessible to the constituents of each district. This could drastically improve the concept of democracy.

The above reasoning applies to our National Congress as well, but there would be so much resistance that I am saving that to be discussed in goals in Section (3) of this book. A similar question should be raised regarding the conduct of the United Nations. Electronic communication system did not exist when the UN was created after WWII. But today adopting and maximizing the capabilities of electronic communications worldwide would create great economic savings for all UN members.

Again only a few of the large Government expenditures are mentioned in this Section (2) have been sited as examples of the savings to be made if brainstorming could, reject old tradition and demand that elected officials really serve and participate regularly with their constituents.

Another very expensive program in our federal Government is our foreign Ambassador system with annual expenditure of tens of billions of taxpayer dollars. And sadly Ambassador assignments are still part of the age-old "political spoils system" used to reward large campaign contributors. Each Ambassador location includes a sizeable building, fully staffed and really is an anachronism representing a centuries old relic. It is just another of those: We have always done it this way! It could and should be replaced by the capabilities of current electronic communication.

# (3)

# IMPLEMENTING—Now for the Hard Part

Let's get on with the Really Big Job, i.e. finding an individual or several individuals with the necessary qualifications in organizational structure, knowledge of history, and a staunch supporter of the principles of democracy as they prepare a report on changes needed to reduce the size, the cost, and hence increase the efficiency of our Government. At this point in time our interest is on our National Government but the findings would inevitably contain recommendations applicable to State and local Government.

We cannot ask Congress to examine itself, so what is next? The person or persons to serve our requirements should have a record of analyzing financial systems, organization and compensation structures, personnel management and the ability to upgrade and maximize the use of electronic communication systems. We have all heard jokes about consultants but for our huge task there are consultants with years of experience in advising International business organizations, with years of experience in analyzing complete systems and then to recommend improving efficiency and economy. Until there is an assessment of these problems, of inter-departmental relationships, it will be hard to avoid piecemeal corrections. Two names that come to mind with the required qualifications and with International records of achievement are McKinsey & Co. of New York City and Booz Allen Hamilton Co. of Boston. My knowledge in this area is limited and more than likely more names of other qualified consultants can be added.

Of equal and possible even more important is "How To Pay The Cost" of this proposed study? Again Congress should not be involved other than to cooperate with whoever is selected to make the study. Fortunately there are people in our Nation qualified to take the leadership for this proposed study because of their interest in their Nation's well being. This brings to mind the plea of Thomas Paine when stationed with Washington's Army in the 1777 winter at Valley Forge. Paine wrote, "Now is the time for men to come to the aid of their Country." Today many people, men and women, are really concerned for the future of our Nation for it may be as dire as the period of the Revolutionary War.

This appeal for help is a new twist in writing a book. I can think of a few names of outstanding leaders that could lead this urgent drive. Michael Bloomberg, Mayor of New York has shown political neutrality that is desirable. Other names that come to mind are philanthropist Peter G. Peterson of the Peter G. Peterson Foundation, and George Soros; each have given assistance to groups around the world in an effort to improve national governments. If you can name others, men and women for this task please do.

These potential leaders could seek funds from Foundations for this proposed study that could become an outline for changes needed and the re-direction of our democracy in the 21$^{st}$ century. This book stresses the need to introduce Public participation in government through Voter Initiative and Referendum. An expert on this is former Alaska Senator Mike Gravel who attempted in 1978 to introduce this concept of a National Voter Initiative in Government but he could not get enough support from members of Congress. Mike Gravel was also a candidate for President in 2008. I suggest he be considered in a group established to update and reform our Government.

It is my belief decentralizing and redistribution of government of much that has been concentrated at the federal level needs to be assigned to the 50 State Governments. This will result in a surge of new ideas and a major reduction in the cost of Government. If the use of our electronic systems is utilized to its maximum capability it is possible Congress could become a part-time job! The redistribution of governing responsibility to the 50 States will come close to removing the power of special interests in our National Government.

For quite some time Congressional activities have resembled a police department, responding after the crime has been committed. However police departments often convict someone whereas Congress never demotes or fires anyone and the status quo continues.

Suppose none of these suggestions materialize; what would be Plan B? Well, we need to continue to rid ourselves of the self-assumed Royalty that has evolved in Congress by eliminating incumbents in the 2010 and 2012 elections. But we need a plan, something to work toward as history shows mass public demonstrations can ultimately become very angry and in time violence may erupt that could provide the seedbed for Fascism. Germany is a good example—a well-educated nation but so oppressed for so long by the revenge inflicted by the WWI Peace Treaty the Germans in desperation accepted Hitler, an unstable individual that was willing to defy the Treaty imposed by the Allies. Hitler had a plan and though it was a bad one it put an end to decades of drifting.

What about the U. S.? How long can U. S. residents wait for a solution to the financial debacle resulting from a Government out of control? If the above suggestions fail to materialize then Plan B is proposed, resembling THE VELVET REVOLUTION approach used by Czechoslovakia and provided a transition from Communism back to democracy. More recently the Asian countries of Georgia and the Ukraine adopted this approach but with less success than the Czechs. Of course as the incumbents are replaced in the 2010 and 2012 elections the Public needs to keep up the pressure on newly elected officials to decentralize the federal Government and return all possible Government activities to each of the 50 State Governments.

As the next few years unfold "We the People" will find our economy has changed greatly due to the removal of Trillions of inflated dollars of debt created by Wall Street banks and the Federal Reserve's role of continuing the Rothschild dynasty. Some old but respected values will reappear once again as individuals and businesses recognize they need to accept responsibility for their own actions. Gone will be the illusionary Rights that prevailed for decades. It will also be recognized that a democracy requires individuals to participate on an equal basis with elected officials through Voter Initiative and the Referendum to insure democracy is maintained. It will not be necessary to re-invent the wheel—the Swiss have provided a good example for us to follow.

Diligence and work will be required but satisfaction and greater safety will be our reward.

\

*Other books by Carlton W. Laird*

Never Vote For The Incumbent
Beware Of Talking Snakes
Direct Democracy
Oh The World Owes Us A Living